GROWING UP

Having a Hearing Test

Vic Parker

Heinemann Library
Chicago, Illinois

www.heinemannraintree.com
Visit our website to find out more information about Heinemann-Raintree books.

To order:
☎ Phone 888-454-2279
🖥 Visit www.heinemannraintree.com to browse our catalog and order online.

Edited by Dan Nunn, Rebecca Rissman, and Sian Smith
Designed by Joanna Hinton-Malivoire
Picture research by Elizabeth Alexander
Originated by Capstone Global Library Ltd
Printed in the United States of America by Worzalla Publishing.

15 14 13 12 11 10
10 9 8 7 6 5 4 3 2 1

Library of Congress Cataloging-in-Publication Data
Parker, Victoria.
   Having a hearing test / Vic Parker.
      p. cm.—(Growing up)
   Includes bibliographical references and index.
   ISBN 978-1-4329-4799-6 (hc)—ISBN 978-1-4329-4809-2 (pb) 1. Hearing disorders—Diagnosis—Juvenile literature. I. Title.
   RF294.P37 2011
   617.8—dc22   2010024193

Acknowledgments
We would like to thank the following for permission to reproduce photographs: Alamy pp. 9 (© NewStock), 14 (© Bubbles Photolibrary), 21, 23 glossary hearing aid (© kavring); © Capstone Publishers p. 17 (Karon Dubke); Corbis pp. 6 (© Ariel Skelley/Blend Images), 7 (© Corbis), 18 (© Patrick Lane/Somos Images); Getty Images pp. 20, 23 glossary operation (David Leahy/Cultura); iStockphoto p. 15 (© Carmen Martínez Banús); Photolibrary pp. 10, 23 glossary expert (Javier Larrea/age footstock), 11 (David Leahy/Cultura), 12 (BL BL/BSIP Medical), 16, 19 (Image Source); Shutterstock pp. 4 (© Monkey Business Images), 5 (© Sean Prior), 8 (© AVAVA), 13 (© Ronald Sumners).

Front cover photograph of a boy having a hearing test reproduced with permission of Getty (Ross Whitaker/The Image Bank). Back cover photographs of an ear reproduced with permission of Shutterstock (© Monkey Business Images), and a school nurse reproduced with permission of Shutterstock (© AVAVA).

We would like to thank Matthew Siegel for his invaluable help in the preparation of this book.

Every effort has been made to contact copyright holders of material reproduced in this book. Any omissions will be rectified in subsequent printings if notice is given to the publisher.

Contents

Some words are shown in bold, **like this**.
You can find them in the glossary on page 23.

What Is a Hearing Test?

ear

You hear sound through your ears.

You can see part of your ear outside your head, but there are other parts inside your head, too.

A hearing test makes sure that all the parts of your ears are working properly.

It will show if you can hear all sorts of low and high sounds.

When Might I Have a Hearing Test?

You may have had a hearing test when you were a baby.

You may have another hearing test when you start school.

Sometimes your teacher, parent, or doctor might think you have a problem with your hearing.

You may have a hearing test then, too.

Where Will It Happen?

Your hearing test may take place
at school.

You may have to go to the school nurse's
room or an office for the test.

Sometimes your family doctor may do your hearing test at his or her office.

Or you might go for your test at a hospital.

Who Will I Meet?

If you have a hearing test at school, someone will come in to show you what to do.

The person will be an **expert** who knows about ears and hearing.

A hearing test at a doctor's office might be done by your family doctor or nurse.

If you have a hearing test in a hospital, you may meet a special kind of doctor.

What Type of Equipment Will I See?

headphones

You may see a machine that makes different sorts of sounds.

You listen to the sounds through headphones.

The person doing your hearing test may have a small tool with an end that fits inside your ear.

The person will look through this to see into your ear.

What Will I Have to Do?

The doctor or nurse will help you put on the headphones.

He or she will ask you to do particular things whenever you hear certain sounds.

When the doctor or nurse looks into your ears, he or she will ask you to sit very still.

This is a way to check that the inside of your ear is the right shape and is not blocked.

Will the Hearing Test Hurt?

It is natural to feel a little nervous about your hearing test.

However, nothing will hurt you.

It can be strange to wear headphones or let somebody look into your ears.

But everything the doctor or nurse does is to help you.

What Happens If There Is a Problem?

Sometimes a hearing test can show that you have a problem with your ears.

You may need to have further tests to figure out exactly what this is.

A doctor might give you medicine for some ear problems.

This can make your ears better again.

What Other Help Might People Get?

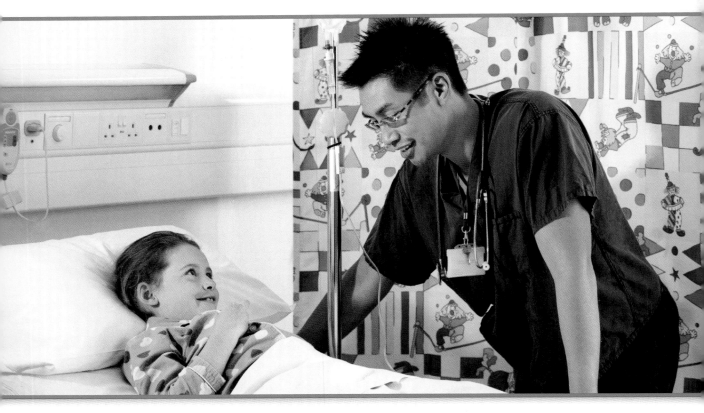

Some people might need an **operation** to solve a hearing problem.

Before the operation, they are given medicine so they do not feel anything.

hearing aid

Some people are given a **hearing aid**.

People wear hearing aids in their ears to help them to hear better.

Tips to Keep Your Ears Healthy

Dos:

✓ Do remember to put sunblock on your ears when you are out in the sun.

✓ Do wear a hat to keep your ears warm when it is cold.

✓ Do remember to dry your ears well after you have been swimming.

Don't:

✗ Don't listen to very loud music.

✗ Don't stick things into your ears.

Picture Glossary

 **expert** someone who knows a lot about something and has special skills in that area

 **hearing aid** tiny machine that fits in your ear, which helps you to hear things better

 **operation** when a doctor fixes problems inside your body. For most operations, the patient takes medicine that makes them sleep

Find Out More

Books

Royston, Angela. *Healthy Eyes and Ears* (Look After Yourself). Chicago: Heinemann Library, 2003.

Stewart, Melissa, and Janet Hamlin. *Now Hear This!: The Secrets of Ears and Hearing* (Gross and Goofy Body). New York: Marshall Cavendish Benchmark, 2010.

Winnick, Nick. *Hearing* (World of Wonder), New York: Weigl, 2010.

Websites

Learn more about taking care of your ears at:
http://kidshealth.org/kid/stay_healthy/body/ear_care.html

Discover more about your amazing ears at:
http://kidshealth.org/kid/htbw/ears.html

Index